Questions & Answers
ANIMALS

First published in 2016 by Miles Kelly Publishing Ltd
Harding's Barn, Bardfield End Green, Thaxted, Essex, CM6 3PX, UK

Copyright © Miles Kelly Publishing Ltd 2016

2 4 6 8 10 9 7 5 3 1

Publishing Director Belinda Gallagher
Creative Director Jo Cowan
Editors Carly Blake, Sarah Parkin, Claire Philip
Designers Fineline Studios, Joe Jones, Sally Lace
Cover Designer Simon Lee
Production Elizabeth Collins, Caroline Kelly
Reprographics Stephan Davis, Jennifer Barker, Thom Allaway

ISBN 978-1-78209-972-7

Printed in China

British Library Cataloguing-in-Publication Data
A catalogue record for this book is available from the British Library

ACKNOWLEDGEMENTS
The publishers would like to thank the following for the use of their photographs:
Front cover Tsekhmister/Shutterstock (duckling), Eric Isselee (orang-utan), mlorenz (tiger)
Back cover Eric Isselee/Shutterstock (gibbon)
Dreamstime.com 51 Steve Byland; 57 and 63(tr) Drpramodb
FLPA 75 Pete Oxford/Minden Pictures; 80 Cyril Ruoso/Minden Pictures
Fotolia.com 19 Judy Whitton; 33 Judy Whitton
iStockphoto.com 58 hilton123; 64 stedenmi; 68 Rawpixel Ltd; 90 smokyme; 93(cr) smokyme
Moviestore Collection 87 Walt Disney Productions
Shutterstock.com 4 Johan Swanepoel; 13 Ilaszlo; 15 Chris Kruger; 21 Leksele; 24 Pal Teravagimov; 33 Leksele;
34 Vladimir Melnik; 36 Kitch Bain; 39 tratong; 40 THPStock; 41 Benjamin Albiach Galan; 43 Kane513; 54 Hedrus;
67 javarman; 69 Vladimir Wrangel; 71 Sara Robinson; 76 Vitaly Titov & Maria Sidelnikova; 83 bobascott;
84 Mike Price; 92 Vladimir Wrangel; 62(bl) Benjamin Albiach Galan; 93(cl) bobascott

All other photographs are from:
digitalSTOCK, digitalvision, Image State, John Foxx, PhotoAlto, PhotoDisc, PhotoEssentials, PhotoPro, Stockbyte

All artworks from the Miles Kelly Artwork Bank

Every effort has been made to acknowledge the source and copyright holder of each picture.
Miles Kelly Publishing apologizes for any unintentional errors or omissions.

Made with paper from a sustainable forest

www.mileskelly.net info@mileskelly.net

Contents

Big Cats

what is the biggest cat?

The Siberian tiger is the biggest cat, and one of the largest meat-eating animals in the world. The heaviest Siberian tiger was recorded at weighing 465 kilograms – that's the same weight as 23 of you! It also has thick fur to help it survive in freezing conditions.

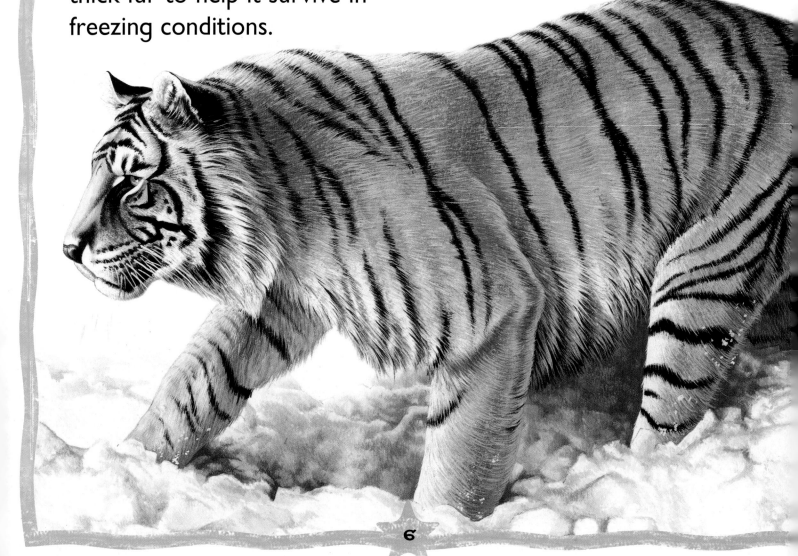

where do tigers live?

Tigers only live in southern and eastern Asia, in forests, woodlands and swamps. They used to live in much larger areas, but humans have now built houses and farms on much of the land. Siberian tigers live in snow-covered forests where temperatures can be -50°C.

Hair-head!

Male lion cubs begin to grow thick fur around their head and neck at about three years old. This fur is called a mane.

Siberian tiger

Why do lion cubs have to leave home?

Male lion cubs don't get to stay with their family group or pride, they get pushed out at about three years old. By then they are old enough to look after themselves. Soon they will take over new prides and have their own cubs.

Discover

Tigers are only found in certain parts of the world. Look on a map and see if you can find them.

what is a caracal?

A caracal is a smaller type of wild cat that lives in hot, dry desert-like places. It hunts small animals, such as rats and hares, and can leap up to 3 metres high to catch a passing bird.

Caracal

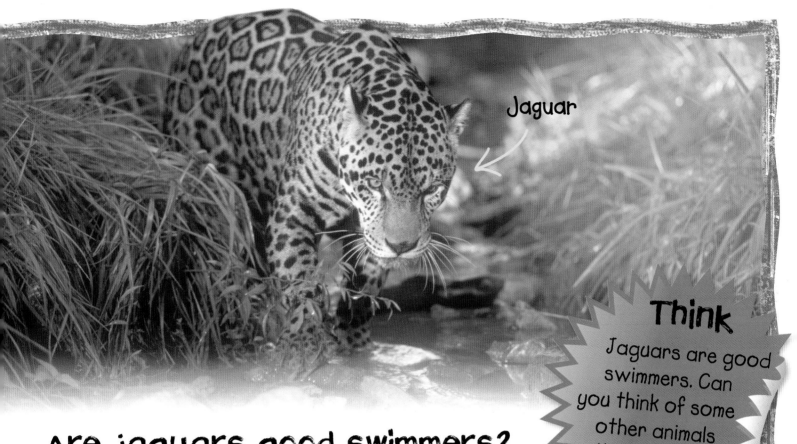

Jaguar

Think

Jaguars are good swimmers. Can you think of some other animals that can swim?

Are jaguars good swimmers?

Jaguars are very good swimmers. Of all cats, they are the most water-loving. They like to live in swampy areas or places that flood during the rainy season, and they enjoy cooling off in rivers. Jaguars are mainly found in Central and South America.

Tiny kitty!

The black-footed cat of southern Africa is one of the smallest cats in the world. It's half the size of many pet cats.

why do tiger cubs have to hide?

Tiger cubs hide behind their mothers for safety. Adult male tigers will kill any cubs that aren't their own. Less than half of the tiger cubs born in the wild live to the age of two years old.

Do big cats live in groups?

Lions are the only big cats that live in large family groups, called 'prides'. A pride is normally made up of four to six female lions, one or two males and their cubs. Some prides may have up to 30 animals if there is plenty of food nearby.

Pride of lions

Pretend

Imagine you are a prowling lion creeping up on your prey. See how slowly and quietly you can move.

which cats can scream?

Small cats such as pumas make an ear-piercing scream instead of a roar. The cat family can be divided into two groups – big cats that can roar, and small cats that can't. A screaming cat can still be just as frightening!

Lady-lion hunt!

Female lions, called lionesses, do nearly all of the hunting for the pride. Male lions will only help with the hunt if it's a big animal such as a buffalo or a giraffe.

Why are lions lazy?

Lions seem lazy, but they have to rest to keep cool in the hot African sun. Usually, lions rest for around 20 hours a day. They normally hunt in the morning or at night when it's coolest. After a big meal they don't need to eat again for several days.

why are tigers stripy?

Tigers are stripy to help them blend into their shadowy, leafy surroundings. Stripes also help to hide the shape of the tiger's body, making hunting easier. White tigers born in the wild are less likely to live as long as orange tigers because they do not blend in as well.

Tiger cubs

Lynx

which cat is in danger?

Lynx numbers are falling because of the drop in the number of rabbits, which are their main food. The Iberian lynx, found in Spain and Portugal, is the most endangered cat. This is because humans have cut down many forests where they live.

what do ocelots eat?

Ocelots, also called 'painted leopards', are small wild cats found mainly in South and Central America. They eat lots of different foods including rats, birds, frogs, monkeys, fish, tortoises and deer.

Think
How many types of food do you eat in a day? Is it as many as an ocelot?

Going, gone!
It's too late for some big cats. The Taiwan clouded leopard, and the Caspian, Bali and Javan tigers are extinct (have died out).

what is the bounciest cat?

The bounciest cat is the African serval. It can leap one metre high and travel 4 metres as it jumps. Unusually, it hunts in the day, for frogs, locusts and voles. Servals are like cheetahs, with slim, graceful, spotty bodies.

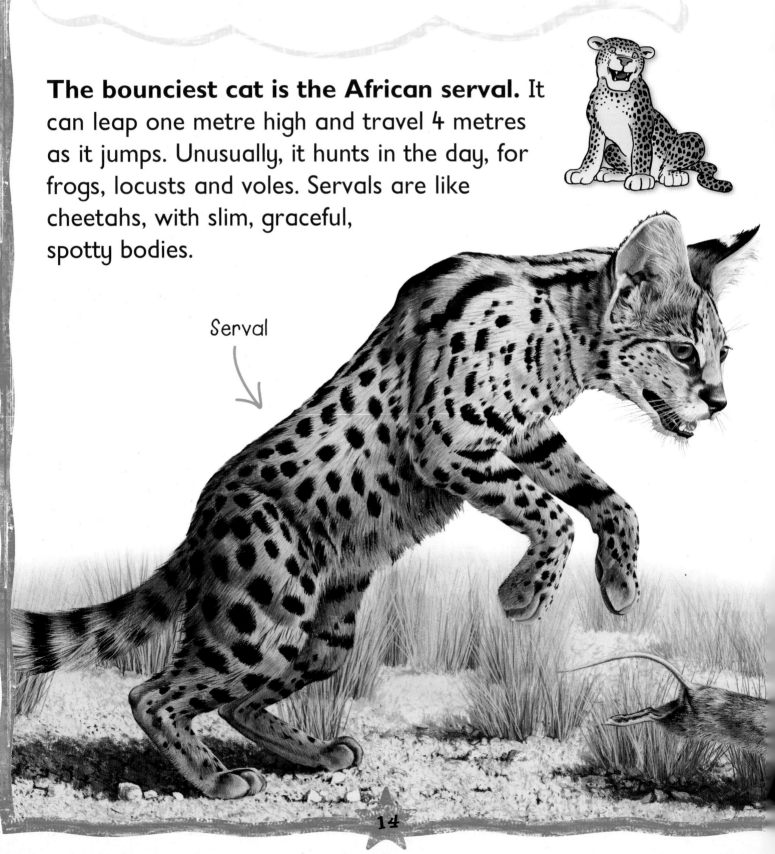

Serval

Do cats change their coats?

The lynx changes its coat with the weather. It lives in forests in northern Europe and Asia. In summer, the lynx's coat is short and light brown, but in winter its coat is much thicker, and light grey. This helps it to hide throughout the year.

Paw prints!

The stripes on a tiger are a bit like our fingerprints – no two animals have exactly the same pattern on their coats.

Why does a lion roar?

Lions roar to scare off other lions that stray onto their patch of land or territory. They also roar to let other members of their pride know where they are. A lion's roar is so loud it can be heard up to 10 kilometres away!

Roaring lion

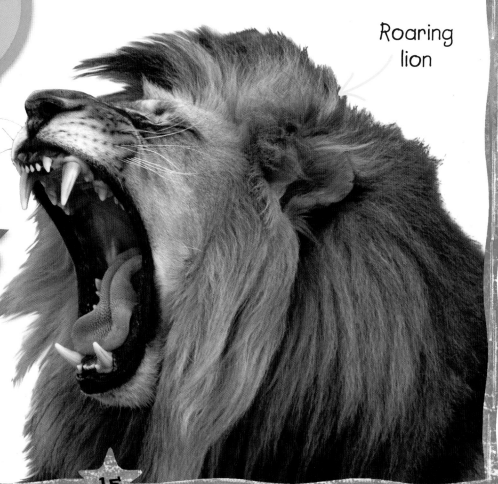

wear

Cats are kept warm by their thick coats of fur. Put on some furry clothes. Do they keep you warm?

Why do leopards climb trees?

Leopards climb trees to rest or to eat their food in safety. These big cats often kill prey that is larger than themselves. They are excellent climbers and are strong enough to drag their prey up into a tree, away from other hungry animals.

Leopard

How can humans help big cats?

Humans can help big cats by protecting areas of rainforest and grassland where they live. These areas are called 'reserves'. In a reserve, trees are not allowed to be cut down and the animals can live in safety.

Puma

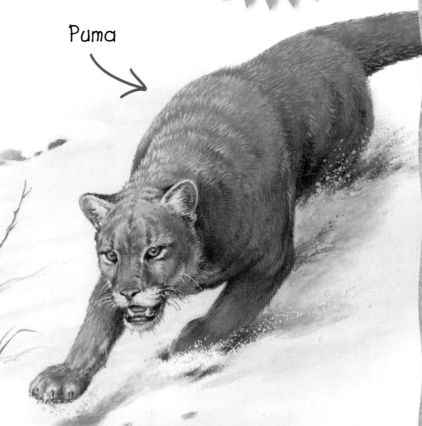

No boat? Float!

Ancient Chinese soldiers used blown-up animal skins to cross deep rivers. They used their mouths to blow in air, then covered them with grease to keep it in.

What is a puma's favourite food?

Rabbits, hares and rats are favourite foods for a puma. They will attack bigger animals too. In places where humans have built their homes near the puma's natural surroundings, people have been attacked by these cats.

can cheetahs run fast?

Yes they can – cheetahs are the world's fastest land animal. In a few seconds of starting a chase, a cheetah can reach its top speed of 105 kilometres an hour – as fast as a car! Cheetahs have 30 seconds to catch their prey before they run out of energy.

why do people hunt big cats?

Mainly for their beautiful fur. For many years, cats have been killed in their hundreds of thousands so that people can wear their skins. Tigers especially were hunted for their body parts, which were used in Chinese medicines.

Make

With a paper plate and some straws for whiskers, make a tiger mask. Cut out eyeholes and paint it stripy!

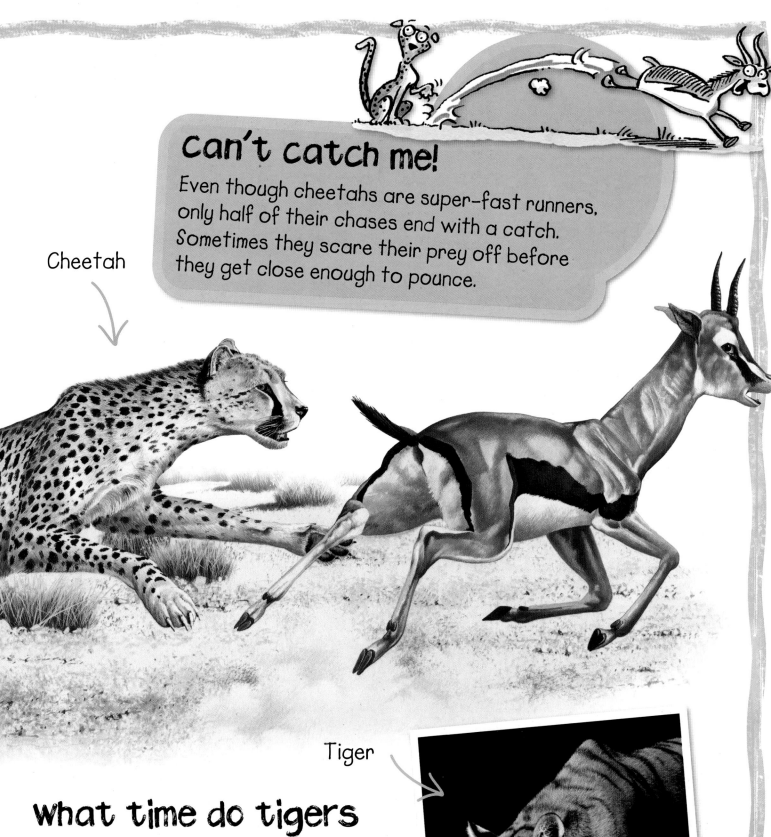

can't catch me!

Even though cheetahs are super-fast runners, only half of their chases end with a catch. Sometimes they scare their prey off before they get close enough to pounce.

Cheetah

Tiger

what time do tigers go hunting?

Almost all cats, including tigers, hunt at night. It is easier for a tiger to creep up on its prey when there is less light. A tiger may travel many kilometres each night while hunting. Tigers hunt deer, wild pigs, cattle and monkeys.

where do cheetahs live?

Cheetahs live in grasslands called 'savannahs'. The savannah is dry, flat and open land, and is home to many other animals including gazelles, wildebeest and zebra. One of the best-known savannahs is the Serengeti in Africa.

Cheetahs hunting in the savannah

why do cats wash their faces?

Cats wash their faces to spread their scent over their body. Cats have scent-producing body parts called glands on their chin. They use their paws to wipe the scent from their glands and when the cat walks, it can mark its area, or territory.

Play

With a friend, collect some pebbles and sticks and use them to mark out your own territories in your garden.

Slow down!

In the wild, cheetahs have a short lifespan. Their running speed gets a lot slower as they get older so they are less successful when they hunt.

How often do tigers eat?

Sometimes, tigers don't even eat once a week. When tigers catch an animal they can eat 40 kilograms of meat. They don't need to eat again for eight or nine days.

21

what is a group of cubs called?

A group of cubs is called a litter. There are usually between two and four cubs in every litter. Cubs need their mother's milk for the first few months, but gradually they start to eat meat. The young of some cats, such as the puma, are called kittens.

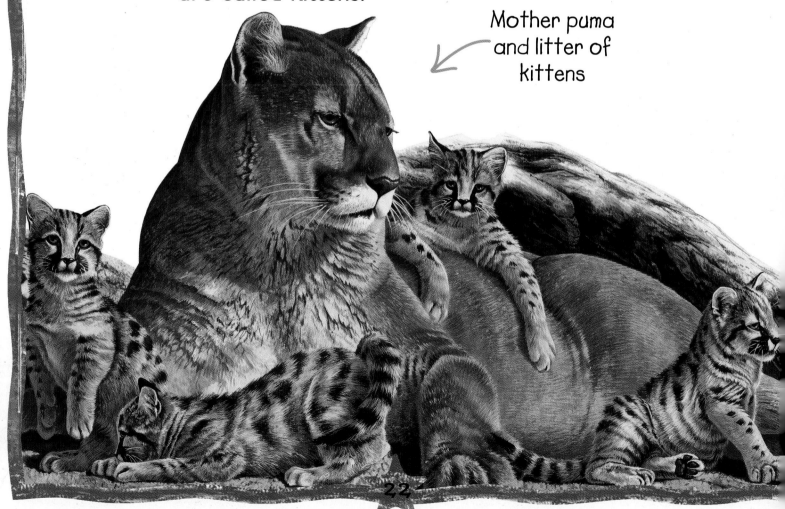

Mother puma and litter of kittens

Sharpen your claws!

Unlike other cats, a cheetah's claws don't go back into its paws. This is why they don't often climb trees – they find it hard to get back down.

why do leopards fight each other?

Leopards fight each other to defend their territory. Each leopard has its own patch of land, which it lives in. Leopards use scent-marking and make scratches on certain trees to warn other cats away.

Leopards fighting

which cat lives in the treetops?

Clouded leopards are excellent climbers and spend much of their time in the treetops of their forest home. These animals have been seen hanging upside-down from branches only by their back legs. Clouded leopards are brilliant swimmers, too.

Draw

Many different animals live in trees. Draw some pictures of animals that live in trees near you.

23

which big cats live in rainforests?

Tigers and leopards live in rainforests in India, and jaguars live in South American rainforests. Here, the weather stays hot all year, although there is often lots of rain.

Jaguar

what animals do jaguars hunt?

Young jaguars climb trees to hunt for birds and small animals. Adults are too heavy for the branches and hunt on the ground for deer, small mammals and sometimes cattle and horses.

Think

Are you as playful as the lion cubs? Invent some new games of your own to play with your friends.

Lion cubs

How do cubs learn to hunt?

Cubs learn to hunt by playing. Even a tortoise is a fun toy and by playing like this, cubs learn hunting skills. Many mothers bring their cubs a small, live animal so they can practice catching it.

It's a wrap!

The ancient Egyptians are well known for their 'mummies'. They even mummified animals including cats, birds and crocodiles.

How do snow leopards keep warm?

Snow leopard

Snow leopards live on snowy mountains in Central Asia. To keep warm in winter they grow a thick coat of fur and store extra layers of fat under their skin. They also wrap their long tails around their bodies when they sleep to keep in heat.

which cat goes fishing?

The jaguar is an expert at fishing. Sometimes it waves its tail over the water to trick hungry fish before it strikes. Jaguars also fish for turtles and tortoises. Their jaws are so powerful that they can easily crack open a turtle shell.

Jaguar

Snowshoes!

Siberian tigers have large padded paws. They act as snowshoes and stop the tiger from sinking into the snow as it walks.

Make

Paint a picture of your favourite big cat. Make it as colourful as you like and give your big cat a name.

How do tigers stay cool?

Tigers such as the Bengal tiger live in places where it gets extremely hot in the summer. They can often be seen lying in pools of water to cool off, or resting in a shady area out of the hot sun.

Which cat is the most mysterious?

The clouded leopard is the most mysterious cat. It is so shy and rare that it is unusual to spot one. Clouded leopards grow to 2 metres in length, half of which is its tail. It uses its tail to balance as it leaps through the trees.

Clouded leopard

why do cats always land on their feet?

Cats have bendy bodies and strong muscles. If a cat, such as a caracal, falls from a tree it can twist its body round so that it can land on its feet. Its muscles and joints take in the shock of the ground for a soft landing.

A caracal lands on its feet

Measure
Using a measuring tape, see if you can measure how long a clouded leopard is.

Big teeth!
The sabre-toothed cat really did exist, about 10,000 years ago. It was the size of a small lion and its teeth were 25 centimetres long!

How many babies do tigers have?

Tigers normally have between two and four babies called cubs. The mother tiger is pregnant for three months, and the cubs are born blind. Most births happen at night, probably because it is safer.

Why are cats the perfect hunters?

Because they have excellent eyesight and hearing, strong bodies and sharp teeth and claws. Many cats, such as lions, have fur that blends into their surroundings, which means they can hunt while staying hidden.

Lion hunting

HOW do cats see in the dark?

Cats have special cells at the back of their eyes that reflect light. They are able to see objects clearly even in dim light, which is why many cats hunt at night. Cats can see four times better in the dark than humans can.

Lioness at night

'Eye' can see you!

Cats have very good eyesight, in daylight and at night. For cats that live in grasslands, this helps them to spot distant prey on the open land.

Try

How well can you see in the dark? Turn off the light and wait for your eyes to adjust. Can you see anything?

Do big cats have enemies?

Big cats don't have many natural enemies. However, they watch out for animals, such as hyenas, that will gang up to steal their meal. A group of hyenas will attack and kill a big cat if it is weak or injured.

Quiz time

Do you remember what you have read about big cats? These questions will test your memory. The pictures will help you. If you get stuck, read the pages again.

page 13

3. which cat is in danger?

page 13

4. what do ocelots eat?

page 6

1. what is the biggest cat?

page 14

5. what is the bounciest cat?

page 9

2. Are jaguars good swimmers?

page 17

6. How can humans help big cats?

7. Why do people hunt big cats?

page 18

8. What time do tigers go hunting?

page 19

9. Why do cats wash their faces?

page 21

10. Why do leopards fight each other?

page 23

page 28

11. Which cat is the most mysterious?

12. How many babies do tigers have?

page 29

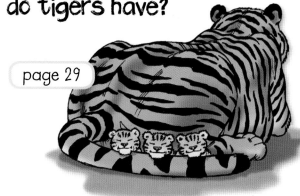

13. Do big cats have enemies?

page 31

Answers

1. The Siberian tiger
2. Yes, they are
3. The lynx – especially the Iberian lynx
4. Rats, birds, frogs, monkeys, fish, tortoises and deer
5. The African serval
6. By creating protected 'reserves'
7. For their fur
8. At night
9. To spread scent over their bodies
10. To defend their territories
11. The clouded leopard
12. Between two and four babies, or cubs
13. No, but hyenas can be a threat

Baby Animals

Which animal is the best mum?

Many animals take great care of their young, but the orang-utan is one of the most caring. They feed their babies for at least three years and cuddle up close every night. A young orang-utan stays with its mum until it is about seven or eight years old.

Baby orang-utan

Big eater!
A baby blue whale drinks nearly 400 litres of its mother's milk every day. That's about five bathfuls!

which frog is the best dad?

The green poison-dart frog is! The male guards his eggs while they develop. Then, after the eggs have hatched into tadpoles, he takes them to a safe pool of water to grow.

Tadpoles

Green poison-dart frog

Find

What did you look like as a baby? Find some photos of you when you were a few months old.

what do baby frogs look like?

Baby frogs, called tadpoles, look very different from their parents. They are little swimming creatures with a tail and no legs. They have gills for breathing in water. As they get bigger, tadpoles grow legs and lose their tail.

Why do fawns have spots?

The spotty coat of a fawn (baby deer) makes it hard to see in its forest home. This is because the sun shines through leaves and twigs, making light spots on the forest floor — just like the spots on the fawn's coat.

Imagine
Pretend you are a mother bird and make a soft nest using blankets and pillows.

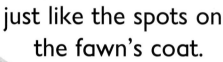

Fawn

How do monkeys clean their babies?

Monkeys groom their young with their fingers and pick out bits of dead skin, insects and dirt. Many animals also lick their babies to keep them clean.

Macaque monkey family

Trunk call

Elephants use their trunks for many things, such as grabbing food from trees. Baby elephants have to learn to control their trunks.

What do baby sharks eat?

Some eat other baby sharks! The eggs of the sand tiger shark hatch inside the mother's body. The first young to hatch then feed on the other eggs. When the sharks are born they are about one metre long.

Why do kangaroos have pouches?

Kangaroos have pouches to keep their babies safe. A baby kangaroo is called a joey and it is very weak and tiny when it is born. It lives in its mum's pouch where it feeds and grows until it is strong enough to look after itself.

Joey

Think

Puppy, kitten, chick... how many other names for baby animals can you think of?

Are turtles born in the sea?

Turtles live in the sea but lay their eggs on land. The mother turtle crawls up onto the beach and digs a pit in which to lay her eggs. When the eggs hatch, the babies make their way down to the sea.

Baby loggerhead turtle

Which animal has the longest pregnancy?

Pregnancy is the word used for the time it takes for a baby to grow inside its mother. The female elephant has the longest pregnancy of any animal – up to 21 months – that's nearly two years!

Watch out!

Family life is dangerous for the praying mantis, a type of insect. The mum is bigger than the dad – and she often eats him!

Why do baby animals play?

Lots of baby animals, such as otter pups, love to play. It helps them grow stronger and learn skills they will need as adults. Play fighting and chasing helps young animals learn how to hunt and catch prey.

Otter pups

which bird makes the biggest nest?

The bald eagle makes the biggest nest of any bird. The largest ever seen was about 6 metres deep – big enough for a giraffe to hide in! The eagles use the same nest every year and add more sticks to it each time.

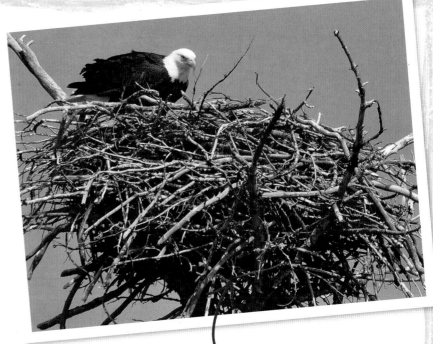

Bald eagle in its nest

Biggest egg

The ostrich lays the biggest egg of any bird. It weighs more than 1.5 kg – that's the same as 24 hen's eggs!

Are baby snakes dangerous?

Some are, yes. Not all types of snake use venom to kill their prey, but those that do, such as rattlesnakes, can give a deadly bite soon after they are born.

Ask
Find out how much you weighed at birth and measure out the same amount using weighing scales.

where do baby rabbits live?

Baby rabbits are called kits and they live in a cosy nest called a warren. The warren is underground and lined with hay, straw and fur to help keep the kits warm.

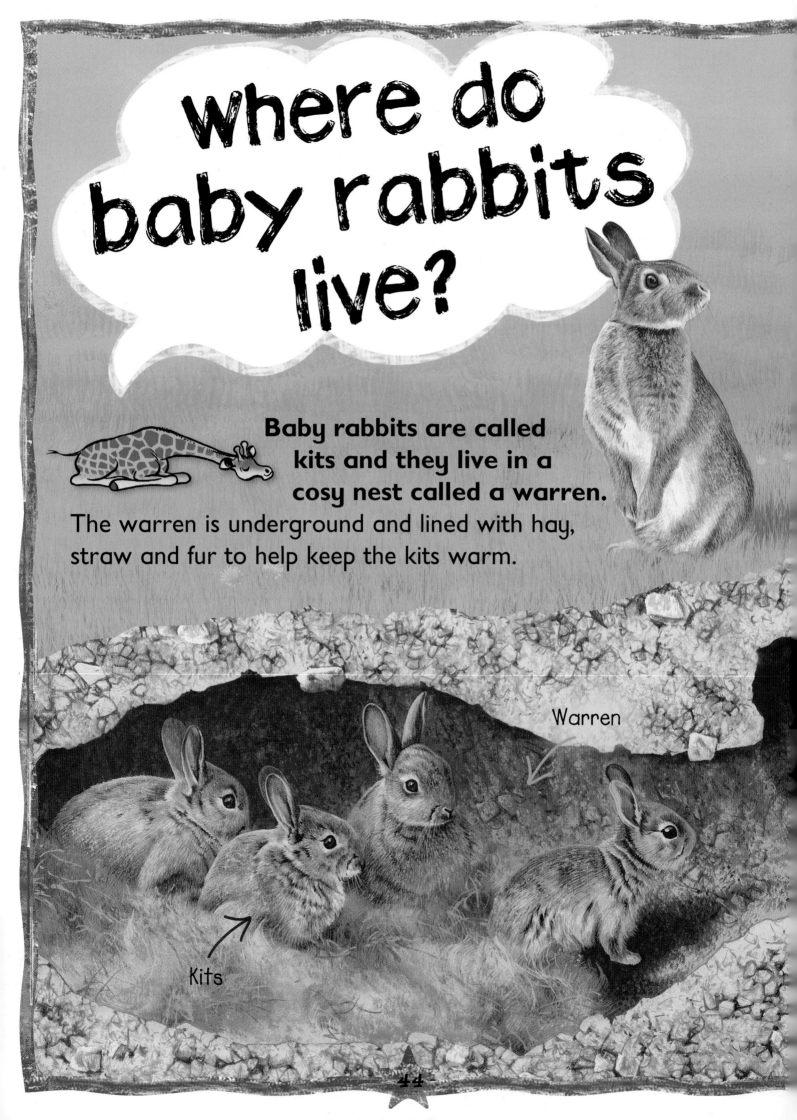

Warren

Kits

when can foals walk?

Just a few hours after they are born! Foals need to be able to walk soon after birth, as in the wild they may have to escape from animals that might hunt them. Foals also stay close to their mums for safety.

Foal

Greedy!

Caterpillars spend all their time eating and can grow to more than 30,000 times the size they were when they hatched!

Draw

What does your favourite baby animal look like? Once you have decided, draw a picture.

Do baby animals laugh?

Some do! Gorillas, chimps and orang-utans laugh when they're playing or tickling each other, just like we do. Scientists think that some other animals, such as dogs, may also laugh.

How do polar bear cubs keep warm?

Polar bear cubs

Polar bears live in the Arctic, where it is always very cold. The mother bear digs a den under the snow where her cubs are born. They live there until they are three months old. It is surprisingly warm and cosy in the den!

Play

Would you be a good mum or dad? Pretend your teddy bear is a baby and look after it carefully all day.

① Caterpillar hatches from its egg

② Pupa is formed

③ Butterfly breaks out of its pupa

when do caterpillars become butterflies?

When a caterpillar has grown as big as it can, it stops eating and makes a hard case around itself called a pupa. Inside the pupa the caterpillar's body changes into a butterfly. The butterfly then breaks out of the pupa and flies away.

④ Butterfly flies away

Big baby

Blue whales have the world's biggest babies. They are about 8 metres long at birth – that's roughly as long as two cars!

Why do scorpions carry their young?

Scorpions carry their babies on their backs until they are big and strong enough to take care of themselves. They climb onto their mum's back when they hatch and are carried around for the first two weeks.

when can squirrels leave their nests?

Baby squirrels are born tiny and helpless with very little fur. They stay in their tree trunk nest for seven to ten weeks, feeding and growing. By ten weeks they are nearly fully grown and can look after themselves.

Mother and baby squirrels

Why do spiders leave home?

Baby spiders are called spiderlings, and as they grow they need to move to new areas to find food. Each spider spins silken threads from the tip of its body. These catch the air like kites and carry the spider to a new home.

Think

Try to think of different animals that make nests and draw pictures of them.

Tall tales

Giraffes are the tallest of all animals. Even a newborn giraffe is around 1.8 metres tall – that's as big as a grown-up person!

Shark egg

Do sharks lay eggs?

Some sharks do. Each egg grows in a strong case, sometimes called a mermaid's purse. The case has long threads that attach to seaweed or rocks to help keep it safe.

Shark pup

Egg case

Do sloths give birth upside down?

Yes, they do! Sloths give birth to their babies hanging upside down from trees! The baby then stays close to its mother, clinging to her fur for the first nine months of its life.

Sloth mother and baby

MAKE

Use some play dough to make a bird's nest and then make some little eggs to place inside.

Queen bee

A queen honeybee lays all the eggs for her hive but she doesn't look after them. The worker bees take care of the babies for her!

How do penguin chicks keep warm?

Penguins usually live in cold places and keep warm by huddling together – the chicks stand on their parents feet. The penguins keep swapping places so each gets a turn at being in the middle – the warmest spot.

Mother bird and chick

How do baby birds get food?

Most baby birds are fed by their parents. Adult birds work very hard to find tasty morsels to bring back to their chicks. The babies always seem to be hungry and wait with their beaks wide open.

Do baby elephants leave their herd?

Only male elephants ever leave their close family groups, called herds. Young elephants stay with their mums for many years. The males will eventually leave and live alone or with other males, but females stay with their herd.

Elephant mother

Calf

Make

Find lots of pictures of baby animals. Stick them on a big sheet of paper to make a poster.

How does a chick get out of its egg?

A baby bird has a tiny spike, called an egg tooth, on its beak. When it is ready to hatch, the chick makes a little hole in the shell with the egg tooth and then struggles out.

Chick breaking out

Egg

Busy mum

Virginia opossums can have up to 13 babies at a time. The babies are tiny at birth and stay with their mum for about three months.

Do badgers keep their nests clean?

Yes they do. Badgers live in underground nests called setts, and use grass, leaves and straw for bedding. The badgers bring their bedding out of the sett to air it and then throw out old, dirty bedding.

Why do lion cubs play fight?

To practise the hunting skills they have learnt from their mothers. Female lions train their cubs to hunt by bringing small animals for the cubs to catch. Then the young lions go and watch their mothers hunting from a safe distance.

Lion cubs
play fighting

① Baby snake breaking eggshell

② Fully hatched

Do snakes lay eggs?

Most snakes do lay eggs, although some give birth to live babies. A snake's eggshell is tough, bendy and almost watertight, unlike a hen's egg. Female snakes usually lay about five to 20 eggs at a time.

Big mouth

The mouth brooder fish keeps its eggs safe in its mouth while they develop and grow.

Why are some eggs pear-shaped?

A guillemot is a type of sea bird that nests on cliffs. Its eggs are pear-shaped with one end more pointed than the other. This shape means that the egg rolls round in a circle if knocked, and won't roll off the cliff.

Paint

Ask an adult to hard-boil some eggs for you. Then paint pictures on the shells.

when do fox cubs leave their dens?

Fox cubs are born blind and helpless so they stay in their dens for the first few weeks. If their home is disturbed, the mother fox may move her cubs to a new den. Most cubs make their first outing when they are four weeks old.

Fox cubs

Why do cuckoos lay eggs quickly?

Because they lay their eggs in other birds' nests, instead of making their own. The other bird then looks after and feeds the cuckoo chick. A cuckoo lays an egg in just nine seconds — most birds take several minutes!

clever baby

A gorilla baby develops more quickly than a human baby. They can crawl at about two months and walk at nine months.

Think

When human babies want their parents they cry. What noise do you think a baby bird makes to get attention?

Which bird has the safest nest?

The female hornbill makes her nest in a tree hole. The male then blocks up the hole with mud so that she and the eggs are safe from hunters. He leaves a hole for her beak so he can feed her while she's inside.

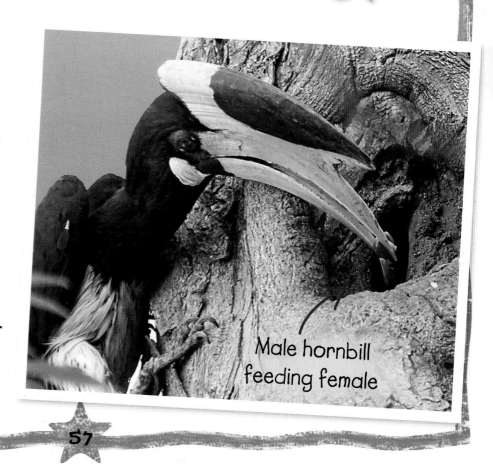

Male hornbill feeding female

when can cheetah cubs live alone?

Cheetah cubs can live alone when they are about 18 months old. Before they are ready to leave their mother they must learn to catch their own food. They learn how to hunt by watching their mother.

Cheetah cubs

Why are harp seal pups white?

Harp seals live in the snowy Arctic. The pups have white coats to keep them hidden from polar bears, which hunt them. Their fluffy coats also help to keep the seal pups warm.

Harp seal pup

What do baby pandas eat?

A baby panda drinks its mother's milk until it is about nine months old. Adult pandas feed on bamboo, and the baby starts to eat this when it is about six months old.

Discover
Some baby wasps feed on dung – animal poo! Find out what some other baby animals like to eat.

Marvellous mum
An octopus is a great mum. She guards her eggs for about a month while they grow, and she doesn't even leave them to find food.

can rhino mums be fierce?

Yes they can – a rhino mum can be fierce when she's looking after her young. If hyenas or other animals try to attack her baby, she charges towards them with her sharp horn to scare them away.

Rhino mum and calf

Are baby hedgehogs born prickly?

Luckily for hedgehog mums, their babies' have very soft spines at first. They harden as the baby grows until they are extremely sharp and strong.

Find out

Ask your parents how old you were when you could first crawl, walk and talk.

Are alligators good parents?

Alligator dads do nothing for their babies, but an alligator mum is a caring parent. She guards her eggs and helps the young to hatch. The mum may then gently lift the tiny babies in her mouth and carry them to water.

Keep warm

The Australian mallee fowl lays its eggs in a mound of earth and leaves. The bird checks the temperature with its beak to make sure its eggs stay warm.

Baby alligator

61

Quiz time

Do you remember what you have read about baby animals? Here are some questions to test your memory. The pictures will help you. If you get stuck, read the pages again.

3. Are baby snakes dangerous?

page 43

4. When can foals walk?

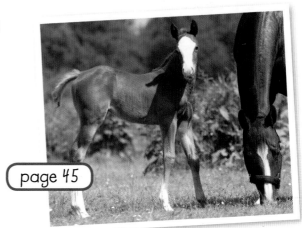

page 45

1. Why do fawns have spots?

page 38

5. Why do scorpions carry their young?

page 47

2. Are turtles born in the sea?

page 41

6. Do sharks lay eggs?

page 49

7. Do sloths give birth upside down?

page 50

page 57 **11. Which bird has the safest nest?**

12. Why are harp seal pups white?

page 59

8. How does a chick get out of its egg?

page 53

13. Can rhino mums be fierce?

page 60

9. Do badgers keep their nests clean?

page 53

10. Do snakes lay eggs?

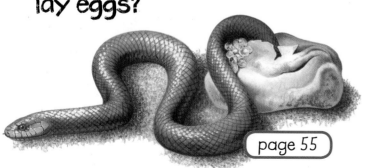

page 55

Answers

1. To help them blend in with their forest homes
2. No, they are born on land
3. The types that have poison are, yes
4. A few hours after birth
5. To protect them from harm
6. Yes, some do
7. Yes
8. Using their egg tooth to make a hole in the shell, then struggle out
9. Yes
10. Most do, yes
11. The hornbill
12. To make them hard to spot in the snow
13. Yes they can – they charge at predators

Monkeys and Apes

what is a primate?

Monkeys and apes are primates. They have big brains and are very clever. Most primates are furry. They have hands with thumbs and fingernails. Humans are primates too.

Spider monkeys

cry baby!
Bushbabies are noisy primates that live in forests. When they make loud calls to each other, they sound like crying babies.

Spell

How many words can you make using the letters in the word PRIMATE?

Are gorillas scary?

Gorillas are usually gentle animals. However they can be very fierce if they have to protect their families. Males can die fighting to save their young.

Do monkeys and apes have tails?

Monkeys have tails, but apes don't. Tails help monkeys to climb and keep their balance. Apes are usually larger than monkeys and they also have bigger brains. Gorillas, chimpanzees (chimps), bonobos, orang-utans, gibbons and humans are apes.

Orang-utan

Do primates stay awake all night?

Nocturnal primates do! Animals that are nocturnal sleep during the day and wake up at sunset. Tarsiers have big eyes to help them see in the dark. They can turn their heads right round, so they can see what's behind them.

← Tarsier

Do bonobos like to play?

Bonobos love to play! Some bonobos living in a zoo play their own game of 'blind man's bluff'! They cover their eyes and try to walk without bumping into things.

Play

Ask a grown-up to help you set up a game of 'blind man's bluff' with your friends.

which lemur has a stripy tail?

Ring-tailed lemurs have long, bushy tails with black-and-white stripes. The males have smelly tails, and when they fight they wave them at each other.

Ring-tailed lemur

Hold tight!

Lemurs run and jump through trees. Babies have to grip tightly to their mothers' fur so they don't fall off!

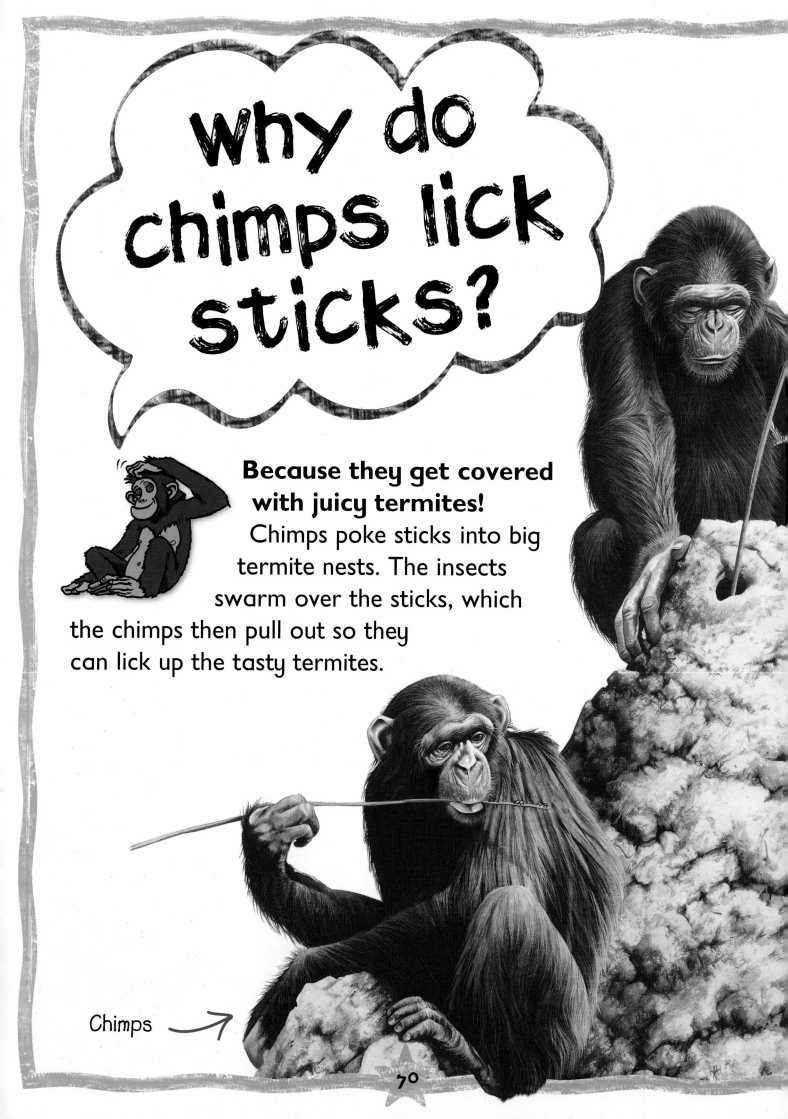

Why do chimps lick sticks?

Because they get covered with juicy termites! Chimps poke sticks into big termite nests. The insects swarm over the sticks, which the chimps then pull out so they can lick up the tasty termites.

Chimps →

Sign

Use the Internet to discover how to sign for 'drink' and 'thank you'.

Greedy monkey!

Barbary macaques have large cheek pouches. When they find food, they stuff it into their pouches and save it for later.

Do chimps like to chatter?

Some do! A chimp called Washoe learnt how to use sign language to talk. She used her hands to make signs for lots of words, such as 'drink' and 'food'.

Why do monkeys sleep in trees?

Monkeys can hide in a tree's branches, so they feel safer in trees than on the ground. Animals that want to eat other animals are called predators. The predators of squirrel monkeys include eagles, baboons and prickly porcupines.

Squirrel monkey

Do apes love their mums?

Yes! All ape babies need their mums to look after them, but orang-utan babies need their mums the most. They stay with their mothers until they are eight years old. That's longer than any other primate, apart from humans.

Orang-utan and baby

why does an aye-aye have a long finger?

An aye-aye has a long finger to get to tasty grubs. These little primates tap trees with their fingers. If they hear a grub moving inside, they make a hole and pull it out with their extra-long middle finger.

Aye-aye

what a racket!

Some mangabeys make a 'honk-bark' noise. Others 'whoop' to call each other and make a 'gobble' sound to say who they are.

why do orang-utans climb trees?

Orang-utans climb trees to play amongst the branches, to find fruit to eat and to stay safe. Predators such as tigers, leopards and crocodiles hunt orang-utans.

Make
Who looks after you? Create them a beautiful card to say 'thank you'.

Why do chimps kiss?

Chimps can be very loving to members of their family. They like to sit together and kiss, stroke and groom each other. If chimps are annoyed they cough, but if they are very angry they bark, cry and scream.

Chimps

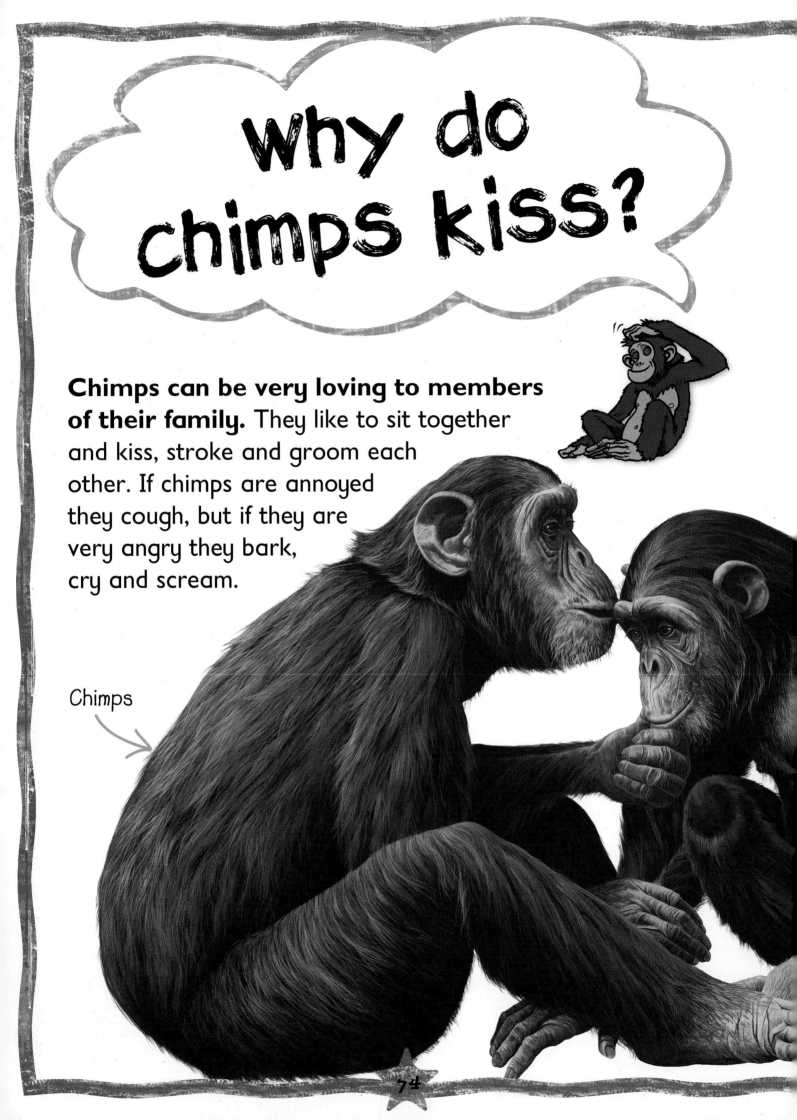

Do primates use tools?

Some primates use tools to help them get food. Capuchin monkeys use heavy rocks to crack open hard nuts. Apes can use tools too, and they even teach each other how to use rocks to open nuts.

Brown capuchin

Time for change!

People love to watch chimps. Sadly, some chimps are taken from the wild to be put in zoos or even sold as pets.

Discover

Use books and the Internet to find other animals that use tools.

when do baboons show off?

Male baboons love to show off when there are females about. They swagger around to show off their big muscles, long fangs and fine fur.

Do primates help forests to grow?

Yes they do! By eating plants and fruits, primates shape the trees and bushes. They also spread plant seeds in their poo. Primate poo puts goodness into the soil and helps new plants to grow.

Macaque →

Why is a slow loris slow?

A slow loris likes to take life at a gentle pace. Moving slowly saves energy, so you don't need to find lots of food. It also helps an animal to stay hidden from predators.

Slow loris

Race

Have a slow race with a friend. The last person to finish is the winner!

Watch out bugs!

Slow-moving primates can creep up on their prey, such as insects, and pounce at the last second.

When do monkeys fall out of trees?

When they get too greedy! Bird eggs are a special treat for primates. Smart birds build their nests on slender branches where monkeys can't reach them.

How fast can a gibbon swing?

Gibbons move faster than any other primate. They can swing through trees at great speed — up to 56 kilometres an hour. Gibbons can cover up to 15 metres in just one swing.

Gibbons

Crab-eating macaque

Do monkeys eat crabs?

Some monkeys will eat almost anything they can find! Crab-eating macaques live in swamps and they will grab crabs and frogs out of shallow water. Sometimes they just drop into the cool water for a swim.

Do primates have hands and feet like us?

Instead of paws and claws, primates have fingers, toes and flat fingernails just like us. This means they can grab hold of branches and delicately pinch small things.

count

If one macaque can catch five crabs, how many can three macaques catch?

super movers!

Spider monkeys are some of the fastest primate climbers. They have very long arms, legs and tails.

which monkey is the biggest?

Male mandrills are the world's biggest monkeys. They are also the most colourful of all furry animals. Mandrills have enormous fangs that can grow to nearly 7 centimetres in length. Males are twice as big as females.

← Mandrill

Why do chimps pull faces?

Chimps pull faces to show how they are feeling. They pout when they want attention, open their lips when they are playful and bare their teeth when they are worried.

Pout

Try out some chimp faces in front of a mirror. Make an angry face too.

Pouting face

Worried face

Play face

Go wild!

Beautiful golden tamarins were once popular zoo animals, but now they are being released back into the wild so they can live free.

Which monkey has a moustache?

Emperor tamarins have big white moustaches. Other tamarins have golden fur, crowns of white hair, beards or hairy ears. Tamarins live in South America.

Do monkeys change colour?

Silvered langurs do! These monkeys have silver-grey fur, but their babies are born bright orange. After three months, grey fur begins to grow. No one knows why the babies are orange, but it may remind older monkeys to be gentle with them.

Silvered langur

Silvered langur baby →

which ape has a colourful bottom?

A healthy male mandrill baboon has a brightly coloured bottom. Their bald bottoms have blue, pink or lilac skin. Female baboons often have pink or bright red bottoms.

A handy tail!

Monkeys use their tails like an extra arm or leg. They can hang from branches using their tails.

why does a sifaka skip?

Skipping is a fast way for sifakas (a type of lemur) to travel. They stand upright, with their arms stretched out, and skip sideways, scooting across the ground. Sifakas stick their tails out so they don't fall over as they hop, bound and leap.

imagine

Pretend to be a sifaka and skip about!

Sifaka

How big is a gorilla?

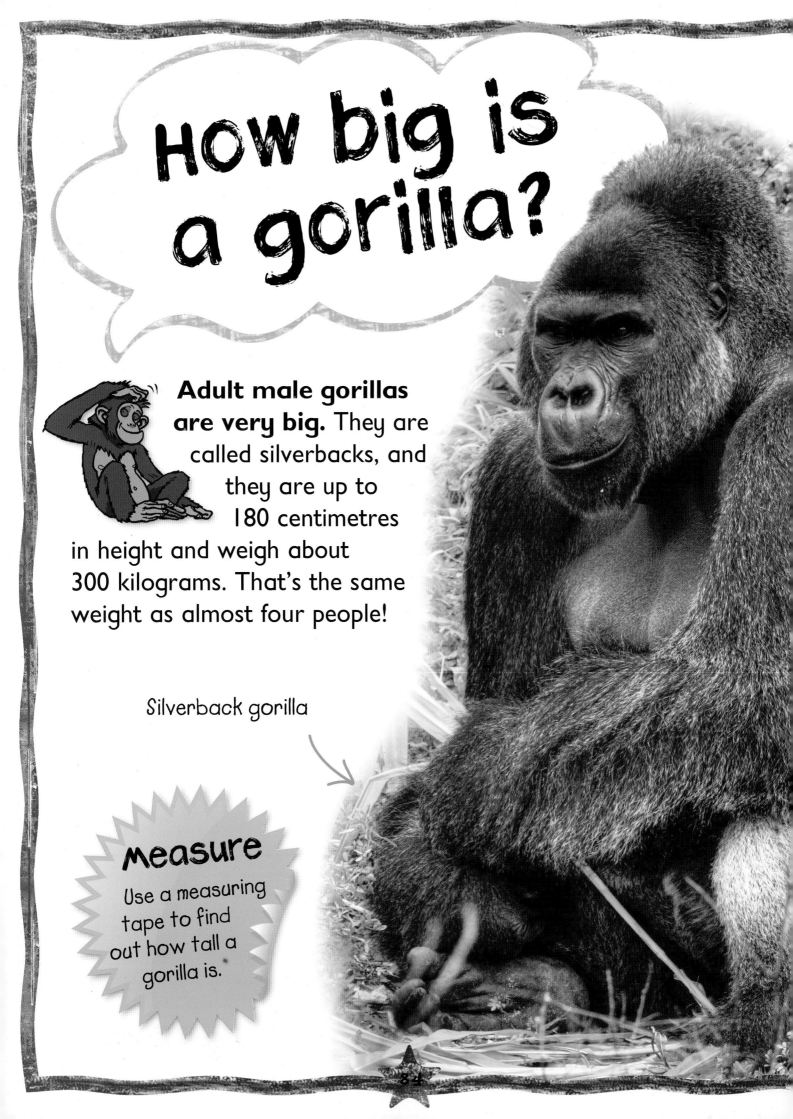

Adult male gorillas are very big. They are called silverbacks, and they are up to 180 centimetres in height and weigh about 300 kilograms. That's the same weight as almost four people!

Silverback gorilla

Measure

Use a measuring tape to find out how tall a gorilla is.

what is the ugliest monkey?

Red uakaris (say: wak-ar-ees) are one of the ugliest monkeys. When they are born, baby uakaris have grey faces, but they turn bright red as they get older.

Bathtime fun!

Suryia the orang-utan lives in a wildlife park. He loved splashing in the bath and was taken to a pool. Suryia can now swim underwater!

Red uakari

why do gorillas beat their chests?

When a silverback gorilla stands up and beats his chest, it is time to get away fast! This is his way of warning you that he is getting angry and might attack.

HOW do bonobos keep clean?

Bonobos spend lots of time cleaning each other's fur. They pick out bits of dirt, dead skin and even insects. This is called grooming and it is an important way for apes to make friends.

Bonobos

Do baboons have manes?

Male hamadryas baboons have large manes of hair that make them look big. Ancient Egyptians thought the silver-white manes made the baboons look sacred, or holy.

Scoop and sip!

Some baboons dig holes by ponds and let water flow into them. The water is clean enough to drink, with no nasty bugs in it.

Think

Can you think of any other animals that have manes of hair or fur?

Which orang-utan is in a film?

King Louie is one of the cartoon stars of a Disney film called *The Jungle Book*. He loves to sing, dance and play practical jokes. The story is based in an Indian jungle, but orang-utans don't really live in India.

King Louie

Baloo

which monkey has a big nose?

In Southeast Asia there are small monkeys with big noses. They are called proboscis monkeys (say: prob-os-kis), because proboscis is another word for 'nose'. The males have the biggest noses of all. When they run, their noses flop up and down!

↖ Proboscis monkeys

Make

Use card and coloured pens to create a monkey mask.

Why do De Brazza's monkeys have white beards?

To scare other monkeys! De Brazza's monkeys also have long fangs. When they open their mouths wide, the white beards and long teeth make them look scary.

De Brazza's monkey

Go ape!

Every year, people all over the world dress up as gorillas and run 7 kilometres. They raise money to save the few gorillas that still live in the wild.

How do orang-utans stay dry?

Orang-utans live in tropical forests where it rains a lot every day. These clever apes use big leaves like umbrellas, and hold them over their heads to keep dry!

HOW do monkeys keep warm?

Most monkeys live in warm places.
Japanese macaques live in mountainous areas where the weather can turn very cold. They keep warm by soaking in pools of hot water that bubble up from the ground.

Japanese macaques

Why do bushbabies leap?

Bushbabies leap to catch their prey. They are fast movers, and can even take scorpions and spiders by surprise. In just one leap, a bushbaby can cover 10 metres!

Think

Can you work out how many metres a bushbaby would cover in three leaps?

Lucky for some!

Only some lucky Japanese macaques have hot springs to soak in. Others have to huddle together to keep warm when cold winds bring snow.

Which primate has two tongues?

Bushbabies use two tongues to eat gum, which comes from trees. They use their teeth to scrape the gum from the bark, then wipe it off their teeth with the special second tongue.

Quiz time

Do you remember what you have read about monkeys and apes? Here are some questions to test your memory. The pictures will help you. If you get stuck, read the pages again.

3. Why do chimps lick sticks?

page 70

4. Why does an aye-aye have a long finger?

page 73

page 67

1. Are gorillas scary?

page 69

2. Which lemur has a stripy tail?

page 75

5. When do baboons show off?

6. Why is a slow loris slow?

page 77

7. Do monkeys eat crabs?

page 79

8. Which monkey has a moustache?

page 81

9. Why does a sifaka skip?

page 83

10. What is the ugliest monkey?

page 85

11. Do baboons have manes?

page 87

12. Which monkey has a big nose?

page 88

13. How do monkeys keep warm?

page 90

Answers

1. Gorillas are usually gentle, but they can be fierce when they protect their families
2. The ring-tailed lemur
3. Because they get covered with termites when chimps poke them into big termite nests
4. To get to tasty grubs in trees
5. When there are females about
6. To save energy and stay hidden from predators
7. Crab-eating macaques do
8. An emperor tamarin
9. Skipping is a fast way for them to travel
10. The red uakari
11. Male hamadryas baboons do
12. The proboscis monkey
13. Japanese macaques keep warm by soaking in pools of hot water that bubble up from the ground

Index